Only
Dark Around the Edges

A Collection
of Poetry and Prose

For ~ Cate ~
If you have a choice,
always...
Be the Poem!
Fiona

Fiona Summerville

DARK AROUND THE EDGES

First Edition

This is a work of fiction. Names, characters, places, and incidents are a product of the author's imagination. Locales and public names are sometimes used for atmospheric purposes. Any resemblance to actual people, living or dead, or to businesses, companies, events, institutions, or locales is completely coincidental.

Copyright © 2016 by Fiona Summerville

www.fionasummerville.com

Dedication

For Cody...

You got this, and I've got you.

Introduction

One rarely gets to know a gypsy's heart much less realize that they've met someone with a true gypsy spirit. They only know if these extraordinary people let them in.

This spirit, this heart, I speak of is made up of pure inspiration manifested into solid form. She breathes in an entire lifetime before every exhale which seems to give permission to the horizon for yet another sunrise. Always looking up even if something of interest brings her gaze downward. Seeking the purest light in any brightness, as well as the loneliest corners in the dark.

She'll accept all things coming her way by good intention, yet recognize shenanigans from a mile away, and often choose not to suffer the cruel ones. Loves harder than any natural order and holds a grudge that fits the crime tenfold.

She can approach unnoticed, never need to interject her thoughts, but always leaves an indelible mark. One that seems to have a time release effect on all those she encounters. Either today, the next, or perhaps years down the road... they will feel her spirit through some moving inspiration.

I know these things, because Fiona befriended me. I am one of the lucky ones she let in.

Poet Darcy, aka Alan Walker

Table of Contents

7

11

- LIFE -

Dark Around the Edges

Tragedy
tinged her world
with sullen shades
of grey and black
but somehow
she always managed
to make it work

never allowing
the darkness
to overshadow
the colors of her life
instead
simply using it
to enhance

like
a black silk scarf
draped gracefully over
solid shoulders
its ends
always trailing in the wind

something
she could take off anytime
but chose not to
leaving her always
a little
dark around the edges

...but she rather liked it that way

Thundering Hope

To me
hope is not a thing with wings
but a magnificent beast
with thundering hooves
charging headlong
through the darkness
towards the dawn

Be Fearless

Intrepid
souls
prevail

The Fixer

She was a fixer...

She patched things up
...made things right
took every mistreated
beautiful heart
and loved them
back to life

that was her gift
and often her burden
...to care
...to feel so much
expecting its
seldom return

She was a fixer
...that's just what she did

The Difference

Every morning she woke
with the singular purpose
of making a difference
somehow
some way
somewhere along the way
even if only one heart was lifted
she rested in the satisfaction
of a task well-completed

She was born to make a difference
and she was the difference
that was made

Bring It

Sometimes life will beat you down
Bring you to your knees
Then laugh as you wallow in the mire
struggling to breathe
But when it asks if you've had enough
That's when you'll slowly stand and say

"Bring it on. I'm just getting started.
You hit like a bitch anyway."

The Mighty Oak

Sometimes
after having weathered
storm after storm
even a mighty oak
needs reminding
his branches can withstand
yet another virulent
attack from forces
beyond his reach
and even if
a few branches give way
when the winds die down
and sun light breaks through
I will see him standing
just as strong and mighty as ever before

No Surrender

Cry
Yell
Scream
Throw things if you must

Be angry
at me
at yourself
at the world

I know you hurt
I know you're tired
of feeling the way you do
all the time

But baby I also know
you got this
and I got you
when you don't

So don't you fucking dare
even think about
ever
giving up

Silent Strength

People tell me:
"You're so strong.
I don't know how you do it.
If it was me I would have crumbled."
I smile and shrug
one platitude or another
when I really want to say

"I'm tired.
I'm weak.
I'm ready to break.
I cry myself to sleep
I hurt all the time...just hurt.
I'm tired and I hurt.

And I hate it...

I hate being sad
Hate crying all the time
Hate this fist of hurt gripping my heart
but most of all I hate
not having anyone to tell."

But for now
I'll live with the illusion I've built
because should there come the day
they face a trial of their own
I want them to remember me
and my supposed strength
and how I didn't crumble
when it got to be too much.

And should they ask
how I made it through
only then
will I tell them the truth

"I was tired.
I was weak.
I was ready to break.
I cried myself to sleep
I hurt all the time...just hurt.
I was tired and I hurt.

And I hated it…

But in that hatred of the hurt
in the tears that flowed every night
I found the strength I needed
to face each day with a smile
and the resilience
to somehow make it through
without crumbling.

And so will you, my friend.
I promise, so will you."

Grace

Never really falling apart
she just tends to crack
a little
here and there
from time to time
yet always masks it with a smile
opting
to let the tears flow
instead
behind closed doors

There is no deception
in her behavior
only quiet strength

and shining under pressure
...that is her grace

Faith

Moments of sunshine
break through
the grey
lingering
just long enough
to remind her
of what was
and will be again

If only her faith
can hold out
until then

Wings

She never tired...

When the soles
of her shoes
wore thin

she found
her wings
and flew

Breaking Free

She thought her heart was breaking
but it was only breaking free

Tear-filled past failures
and painful regrets
crumbled to dust

Until all that remained
was hope
renewed

...and ready to take flight

Rebirth

In order to grow
I had to crumble
Lay dormant
...listening
Conversing
with the silence
and the shadows
surrounding me
Learning
...quietly rebuilding
Finally emerging
stronger
braver
and just a bit wiser
than before

Don't Call Her Pretty

She never wanted to be thought of
as beautiful
or pretty
Those girls always ended up
seemingly untouchable
The burden of their façade
an eventual prison
the walls of which they fought
valiantly
and vainly
each day
to stay locked behind

No...
she didn't want to be thought of
as pretty
or sweet...
or nice...
She had too many cracks
and sharp edges
...too many odd
and off color thoughts
to bear the burden
of that designation with any integrity

She didn't want to be thought of
as any of those things.

She just wanted to be thought of
by someone
...anyone

with love
...period

And So She Ran

And so she ran...

Headlong
arms outstretched
into the familiar darkness
that forever beckoned her to return

It wasn't home
but it was close

A place
she knew to go
to lose herself
deep within
the chaos
of its dark embrace

and maybe
...just maybe
to find a part of herself
she'd lost
somewhere along the way

The Dark

She wasn't afraid of the dark...

It's where her soul burned the brightest
and her demons
could bask in its glow.

Stars

As night descended
she glanced up and smiled
thankful for all the stars
littering her night sky

...especially those broken dreams
and shattered promises
now turned
to tiny glittering beacons of hope

for those were the ones
leading her home
and ever closer
to her truth

Right Place

Broken dreams
fateful twists
and outcomes
aside

She nurtured her wild spirit
let her heart run free
following it
wherever it led her to be

Trusting she'd find herself
exactly where
she was meant to be

...at precisely the right time

The Universe Within

The quieter you become
the more you hear...
Just stop
for a moment
be still
and listen

Listen
to the gentle whispers
of longing from your heart
to the soft murmurs
of truth
from deep within your soul

Listen well
and trust them
it's the Universe speaking
...and you
my lovely heart
are the Universe

Silence

Never fear
the dark
silent moments
of your mind

...it's the only time
the truth
doesn't have
to roar

Don't Give Up

Don't settle
Don't slow
Don't let the Can'ts and the Won'ts
overwhelm your Will

Feed the flames of your desires and dreams
with kindling made from
the dead and rotting carcasses of
Never Wills and Don't Bothers

Your life is a blank canvas
paint yourself a masterpiece
filled with vibrancy and color
to encourage and inspire

You might stumble
make mistakes
but that humanity just makes
your life all the sweeter

Just don't give up
...don't you ever give up

Just Love

When my time on earth
comes to an end
and I'm asked
what I think my proudest
accomplishment to be
I'll smile wistfully
and softly say…

"I loved
…just loved
I loved it all
and loved it well
be it man or woman
foe or friend
or creature feathered or furred
I gave all a chance
and all the love I had
sometimes even more
I lived to love
and relished every moment;
even the most painful times
most would choose
to bury or forget

As for regrets
I have just one...
that I didn't try to love
the ones
so filled with hate
a little more
because
truth be told
they were the ones
who needed it
...the most"

Art

Let your struggle
become your art

The Muse

The role of muse to a writer
is one aspired to by many
but often realized only by
the most unassuming ones

Those who understand
the chaos
and dark despair
within which the writer sometimes dwells
and aspire only to soothe
not be written into a poem of epic unrequited love

Those who can ride
hands free
up in the air
on the writer's roller coaster
of emotion and pretty words
anticipate the steepest drop
and be there to break their fall

And…

By those who don't need to be reminded
that a writer's passion is not simply inspired
by a pretty face or feckless lust
but by those genuine ones
who touch their soul
in ways no others can

Hot Poetic Mess

On a good day
I'm a mess...
a sound orderly mind
at constant war
with an unruly soul
that plays home
to broken poems
and orphaned words
stumbling
each over the other
jostling
for attention
as they spill out
onto the page

Write On

Don't shrink silently into the night of tales left untold

Write
until it hurts
and then write more
until that ache is soothed

Write until you've wrung yourself
Hung yourself
Until you're empty
and no more

Remembering the measure of success
lays not
in the recognition and adulation
of the throngs

but in the one heart
shifted
lifted
or illuminated

by the musings of your restless soul

Morning Pages

Morning stillness...
thoughts yawn
and stretch out
across the page
slowly
untangling themselves
from sweet nocturnal wanderings
before leaping headlong
into a steaming
hot cup
of sunshine and hope

Intelligence is Sexy as Fuck

Don't underestimate the seductive power of a decent vocabulary.

Don't be afraid to learn and use fabulously, juicy words. Not slang, or lazy acronyms (see YOLO or BAE.)

Real words.

The diamonds and rubies of the dictionary and thesaurus.

Learn what they mean and use them.

Frequently.

And for heaven's sake, under no circumstances are you to let anyone tell you that you must dumb down your writing or vocabulary in order to be understood. If they do, chances are they're intimidated, and just too lazy to expand their narrow minds and obviously limited vocabulary. The onus falls to them, not you.

Remember, pretty is nice, but looks fade.

A well-educated, well-versed woman is, and will always be, a force to be reckoned with.

Intelligence is power.

Intelligence is sexy as fuck.

Wine, Words and Song

Strive to live a life rich and replete

Filled with music...
brimming with beauty...
heady with intoxicating words
and wine

...there should always be wine

- LOVE -

Safe Harbor

To love the one
who settles you
who calms your soul
who lifts your drowning spirit
with little more than a word
who offers you safe harbor
when the storms
internal and external rage
...is easy

It's finding them
and falling asleep
in the shelter
of their embrace each night

...wherein the difficulty lay

Souls

Meet me
on the edge of forever
where your darkness melds with mine
and the missing pieces of our souls
will find each other once again

Simple Heart

A knight in shining armor
may look good on paper
but they tend to rust away
when the storms
within and around me rage.

Instead give me a warrior
battle worn and true
Who'll fight beside me
...with me
and for me

Standing steadfast
naked
and undaunted
in the eye of the hurricane
I can become.

A real man
made of flesh
...of blood
and honor...
nothing mythic or contrived

just
a simple heart
asking nothing of me
in return
...but love

The Master Craftsman

Tirelessly he worked
layer by layer
stripping away
her battle worn armor

Endlessly smoothing
the rough
frayed edges
of her heart

Paying special attention
as he buffed
to the scars
etched deep into her soul

Until her eyes
reflected back
the devotion
he'd poured in

A craftsman's masterpiece revealed
her true beauty reemerging from within

Indian Summer

Wild and free
She blew in
on the
Indian Summer breeze
and flowed
like a river of hope
soft and easy
over Him

Washing clean
the dirt
and tawdry remains
of a dust storm
filled with lies
and shallow intent
and gently buffing pain's
jagged edges away

Until
once again He stood
steadfast and gleaming
the strength and character
of a thousand generations
on display
for all the world
to see

The Wish Come True

I wished for you, you know…

A broken soul's whispered plea
carried across the night sky
on the moon's silvery beams

Dreamt of you...
your touch
your kiss

Knew you...
loved you
long before

I ever saw your face

Almost Too Late

Almost too late
he realized
she'd always been there
holding vigil
filling the silent moments
and down beats
within the darkest shadows
of his heart
with whispers of hope
and pouring
love
unconditional
into
the most broken parts
of his soul

Precious Gems

To Him
She is an angel
pouring love into cracks
long neglected
and widened
by the others
...a southern breeze
gently blowing
melting the permafrost
slowly encasing his heart
...who cradles
His soul
as if it were
the most precious
gem on earth

But that's not how
she sees herself
...no not at all
when she looks in the mirror
She sees only a girl
hopelessly in love
with a man
better than the rest
more deserving than most
of a life complete
...who cradles
Her soul
as if it were
the most precious
gem on earth

Guiding Light

After so much wasted time
spent in the dark
and
all alone

Her love
was a welcome
soft yet constant
guiding light

leading him to shelter
...beckoning him home

Stay

Stay
Don't move just yet

Let's linger here
warm in bed
bodies entwined
as the day dawns around us
for just a while longer

Let your fingers
follow the path
of the first ribbons of daybreak
as they fall across my body
in soft, hazy hues of pink and gold, warming
touching
slowly igniting
the languid need
laying dormant
just beneath
the lazy trail of your caress

Awaken me slowly
with kisses
and murmured petitions
of love
as sweet
as the lilting melody
of the cardinal perched
just outside our window

Rise above me
roaring to life
like a lion

bathed in the golden rays
of morning's first light
impaling me
driving deep
reawakening the desire
not long sated
from the night before

Let the sounds
of our love
mingle
with those
of the dawning day

Until once again
we linger
warm in bed
bodies entwined
as the day dawns around us
for just a while longer...

Work of Art

This bed was nothing more
than a blank and empty canvas
until the day we laid upon it
made love on it
transforming it
with feverish strokes
into
a priceless work of art

The Poem and Her Poet

Their story began the moment he found her...

She...
like words free floating
in search of poetic meaning

He...
the poet on a quest
in search of his poem.

Interpretation and meaning
making sweet love

Beautiful

He whispered,
"My God you are beautiful"

And for once
she finally believed...

because
reflected back
within his eyes
she saw her soul
engulfed
in love's pure flame
and wrapped
in dreams of what might be

Breathe

While others only tried to take my breath away...
You taught me to breathe

Passionately Profound

Ours
is an easygoing
togetherness
Quietly enduring
Passionately profound

We find comfort
in the lingering silences
occupied only
by soft sighs
and beating hearts

Where the Mind Goes

Wandering thoughts
always
led to him

Bliss

Despite the unrelenting darkness
and cacophony of restless souls
crying out
for attention
redemption and release
their souls met
collided
and merged

Bleeding out
each into the other
Becoming
one unto the other

Earthbound by the mundane no longer
they soar high above the distracted din
on passion's fiery wings
before coming to quiet rest
upon a downy bed
of whispered hope

No more chaos
only promise
No more sorrow
only bliss

If I Were Your Truth

If I were your truth
impassioned fingers would seek out
every seed of doubt you've ever buried
one by one
laying them to rest
in the field of Nevermore and Forgotten

My whispered kisses would convey
the answers to every question
too long unanswered
setting all others free
to blow away on the warm Summer breeze

And my body would be both vault and key

For the sweetest truths
yet to be learned
remain locked away

...in me

The Other Me

Don't fall in love with my smiles and whimsy

Fall for my quiet moments
the pensive and reflective ones
Those times I'm so lost within anguish
I could easily fade away

Those are the times
when I'm most myself
and need your love
to see me through

Please...
fall in love with that me first
If you can
I know you'll stay

Ruined

She thought herself ruined
...broken
in all the places
most never
bothered looking
Then he arrived
and quietly
...without asking
combed through the clutter
digging deep
until he found her
and loved her
back to life
...ruined places
dusty spaces
and all

Kintsugi

You took me at my most broken...
filled
the empty gaps
and fissures
with gold
until
I stood
before all
once again whole
...stronger
and more beautiful
than before

Whispers of the Heart

He'd told her once
he carried her
in every breath
and downbeat of his heart
and now
as she rested her head
she couldn't help but smile
hearing
every "I love you"
she'd ever whispered
echoing softly
in his chest

Ritual

He's the nightly prayer
falling softly
from her hungry lips
and her morning mantra
upon waking,
longing for his kiss

Thank you

Every time I think of us
my mind stutters and stalls
leaving my heart's desires trapped
and at the mercy
of my fumbling finger tips
to set them free

Most times
they elucidate my feelings
in a most enchanting way

Sometimes, though
gold woven words fall hollow
leaving little else to say
but

I love you
and thank you
for finding
and making me yours

Never In Vain

No time
...no love
is ever wasted

one
perfect moment
shared
with another
imperfect heart
a treasure
imprinted
...to be cherished
created
in the time it takes to blink
and while
time and space
continue
their never-ending race
that one moment
will remain...
perfection
frozen
...and never in vain

The Heart of a Warrior's Wife

They parted in the rain. Their bodies melding together in a tight lingering embrace neither wanted to break. Lips brushed, longing filled gazes locked, and as she watched him drive away, she beamed a bright, happy smile his way. Not until his car turned the corner did she let the drops of her breaking heart stream down her cheeks to mix with the summer rain.

Now, not a day goes by in which the deep timber of his voice doesn't weave its way in and out of her thoughts. She feels his lips on hers, his hands caressing and stroking the small of her back. She sees his wry smile and quirked brow staring at her bemusedly.

She wakes up missing him, and ends her day the same. Smiling and laughing her way through the hours in between. Never letting on to the world the true state of emptiness she feels with him gone. The heart knows what the heart wants, regardless of the dictates of the universe and everyday life.

His name is a silent prayer on her lips every night before her eyes close, a morning affirmation upon waking. Praying for her warrior's safe return to their home and to her arms once again.

How Do I Love Thee

It's simply not possible for me to put into words how I feel about you. The attempt would be feeble and no doubt trite. I'd be forced to put boundaries on something that has none. Describe the indescribable. Define that for which there are no adequate words.

Platitudes, yes.

Euphemisms, most definitely.

Words, no.

I suppose I could wax poetic in a "how do I love thee" sort of way, but there again, I'd be forced to enumerate the how and why of my love for you, and I just can't.

Because, it just is.

It's as natural and unconscious as the breath I take. Something I've always done, and always will. Well, at least until, you know… that whole death thing happens. But even after my last exhale, I'll still love you.

What I feel for you can't be confined to one plane of existence. Like our souls, it's endless. A boundless, never fading nucleus of energy and light. Nurturing and guiding the way from this life to the next.

Yes, I do believe in soul mates, and reincarnation. I believe we "run" with the same group of souls in each lifetime. They may never play the same role, but they're always there.

Teaching, learning, growing, evolving. Constant.

Were we lovers in a past life,
and will we be lovers in the next?

That I can't be sure of. I can only be certain that the
love I have for you will always be there,
regardless of the relationship.

Our paths will cross, the bond will form, and the love
will manifest, just as it has in this lifetime.

I loved you then.
I love you now.
And I will love you always.

Unconditionally.
Steadfast.
Evermore.

Becomes My Story

-collaborative work with Alan Walker-

Her skin like parchment
at the end of my eager lips

Every single shared kiss
erasing all
unrequited heartaches
I had ever written of

And in our embrace
she becomes my story
Reinvented
and epic in its retelling

Never again
would I allow her
to simply read my words
because forevermore

... she is the poem

- LUST -

Needful Things

Our story was comprised
of too many late nights
and too much good wine

Two kindred souls
in two separate worlds
in varying stages of nakedness

Reading poems
talking dirty
and touching ourselves
the way we imagined
the other might
to sate the fire
slowly building
in that needful place
between our thighs

Dark Rebellion

She played the role
of sunshine and sweetness
but when their lips met
her secret was revealed
and oh how he found himself
addicted to
the taste of dark rebellion
in her kiss

Blue Flowers

She wanted
blue flowers
and tender nothings
whispered
as she lay tucked
in a sheltering embrace
when the world
was still and dark

But more than that
she wanted
the lace from her hips
to be shredded and ripped
by a mouth hungry
and hell bent
on tainting
her romantic ideals

...leaving them
drowned in debauchery
and dripping with lust

Secret Aches

Tell me
of your deepest desires
those precious
dark hungers
you keep hidden
from the world

Breathe them
softly over my soul
on the sigh
of an expiring kiss
they're safe with me
as is your heart

I want nothing more
than to know you
to taste your wants
...savor them
and to feel
your most secret aches

...as surely as my own

Ready

Silently
she waits
anticipation rampant
salacious thoughts
his steel
her silk
leave her quivering
primed and ready
for his touch

That Thing You Do

Where did you learn to do
that thing you do
with your lips?

You know
what I'm talking about...

That thing
where you set
my soul aflame
with promise filled whispers
and a trail of velvet kisses
across my skin

Sweet Addiction

He was addicted to
the taste of chaos
in her kiss

Bad Habit

She had a habit
of worrying
her bottom lip
...said
if she bit down
hard enough
sometimes...
she could still taste
his kiss

Sated

Unwrap me
slowly
savoring
every inch of silken skin
every coveted dark desire
exposed

Lay me bare
before you
I am hungry
Unafraid
Unabashed with yearning
to please

Until we collapse
unraveled
yet tangled
desire sated
...abated
for now...

Freedom

With him
her unquiet mind
quieted
thoughts laid down
then dissipated
with every brush of his lips
across her brow

Every tug
of his fingers
knotted in her hair
freed her tangled soul
to soar high
and above
their writhing forms

Pulsing
against crisp white sheets
in desperate search
of another form
of peace and freedom
altogether

Forever

Stay here with me…
Inside of me
Forever

Stripped

Starting with her mind
he stripped her bare
word by sensual word
...button by tiny button
until all that was left
was the sheer lace of desire
covering her soul

...and that fell away
on whispered
innuendo alone

Subtle Chaos

Theirs was a subtle chaos
Non-disruptive
to the universe at large
but, oh what havoc
one simple kiss wrought
within their two colliding worlds

Passion's Cry

Take me
here
now
as we transcend
to that needful place
known
to us alone

Elevate us both
until we run
forever free
endlessly answering
the primal cry of passion
known
to our bodies alone

Ash

Aching
wild and writhing
she bows beneath his touch
a body in search of release

her body hums
as his lips trail kisses
over every wanton curve
seeking her sacred fertile ground

Appeasing
but not sating their needs
he laps greedily
at her pool of primal desire

Her hips and bated gasps
perfectly in sync with each swirl
of his masterful tongue
as he edges her ever nearer to her undoing

Finally rising
bearing down
steel sinking deep
into silken heat

Unrelenting
until they quench that fire from deep within
melting down in form
into a heap of pleasured ash

Lust

Ravenous lust
impervious to propriety
demands release
anytime
any place
and by any
necessary means

Altar

Ardent devotion
allowed for nothing less
than his unadulterated worship
at the altar of her soul

Intoxicated

Lust sipped
from eager lips
is the most
potent intoxicant

The Alcove

Your touch
so heated
yet so fleeting
leaves me longing
for another stolen moment
in that alcove
in the rain

When lace and inhibitions
were stripped away
by hungry lips and fingers
seeking
a warm shelter of their own
daring...
even urging
desire's flood
to wash over them

Dark Paradise

Sanctuary
was found dwelling deep
within the flames that fueled her passion
often
to the point of madness

A fiery chaos within which
he'd risk all
just to dance with her demons
and be relentlessly branded by her dark desires
time and again

Even if it meant
only smoldering ashes
were all the legacy that remained
of his descent
into Paradise

Hidden Things

The dark gleam
with which
he pinned her,
screamed

he knew
and understood

the spoken
...the unspoken
the pauses
and in-betweens
her moments of truth
and ugly hidden things

He understood her everything
but more importantly

he adored her
for all she was
and all she wasn't
not caring
to change a thing

Cravings

And as she stared
into the furious desire
burning
in his eyes
she found herself
unafraid

In fact
his
was just the sort of fury
she needed
...just the sort of darkness
she craved

Sin

You're
my favorite flavor
of Sin

The Beast

Tonight
There is no room for gentle
Take me hard
Take me deep
Rock the heavens with my screams.
Use me
Devour me
Take possession of my soul
Lay claim to this feverish body
aching for release

I love the gentleman you are...
but tonight
I crave the beast

Anticipation

Eyes shrouded in silken darkness I wait...

I've no idea what you have planned,
but knowing
I'd do anything for you
...anything at all

makes the want
...all the greater...

the anticipation
...all the sweeter...

the ache
...all the deeper...

I hear you...
my breath catches

I sense you...
and the need within me grows.

The metal rasp of a zipper
beckons me
I lean forward wantonly
tongue darting out
to wet eager lips

"Open your mouth, beauty."

Your whispered growl
tears a hole in the silence
sending a shiver
of delicious anticipation
surging

And with the tiniest of smiles
tugging
at the corner of my
ready mouth

...I obey.

Two Heads

"Well Kitten, what should I do with that mouth of yours?"

The full implication of his question turned her body molten. What should he do with her mouth? All sorts of deliciously wicked ideas were dancing through her head at the moment, but she was more than willing to listen to his suggestions.

Silently, she crossed the room, the heat of his dark gaze fueling her desire even more as it raked over her and came to rest upon her lips. When she came to a stop before him, she paused for a moment before dropping to her knees.

A knowing, almost challenging smirk slowly spread across his face, as she took the glass from his hands, and sipped.

Her eyes locked with his over the rim of the tumbler. Her body ached for his branding touch, her mouth watered in anticipation of his taste. She wanted nothing more than to free him from the confines of his pants to show him exactly what she should be doing with her mouth, but she would wait...for now.

Or maybe not...

Spurred on by her growing need, and possibly the contents of the glass, she set the tumbler aside, licking a stray drop of the liquid courage from her lips as she nestled herself between his knees. Her head slowly dipped closer and closer to the now very apparent bulge behind the zipper of his trousers, and she gasped softly in wicked anticipation, before smiling up at him slyly.

"I don't know, Sir. But I'm sure if we put our heads together, we might come up with something."

Midnight Delight

She awoke in a tangle of bed linens and body parts. Beside her, his steady rhythmic breathing told her he was asleep, while his hand, cupped possessively around her breast told her what she already knew. She was his.

A soft sigh of contentment passed her lips as she felt herself drifting off once more. Until he gently tweaked her nipple between his thumb and forefinger. The stubble from his chin scraped along her shoulder as his lips sought out and claimed her ear lobe in a playful nip. Smiling into the pillow, she rocked her hips back into his, causing his already hard cock to pulse against her backside.

A low, sleepy growl was the only warning she had before she found herself beneath him, staring up into his hooded emerald eyes. She reached up and brushed an errant wave from his forehead, before pulling him down and capturing his lips with hers in a languorous kiss.

Tongues dueled, teeth nipped and hands gently explored as soft moans and pants filled the room, until the need between them simmered and boiled over. He eased into her then, slowly filling her waiting heat, inch by inch. She rolled her hips into him, silently begging him for more, and cried out when he gave it to her.

Their leisurely pace became frenetic. Her walls tightened around him as he drove into her, forward and back, in an unyielding rhythm. His fingers dug into her ass cheeks, grinding deeper into her as her hips danced wildly against his, sending her headlong over the edge.

Her body exploded around him, and his thrusts became relentless. Their names became a passionate mantra on each other's lips as their cries cut through the silence of the room.

His body collapsed atop hers for a moment, before rolling over and bringing her with him, laying her across his chest, his cock still buried deep inside her warmth. He held her tight, as silence, once again, fell around them.

A warm sense of peace settled over her like her favorite snugly blanket, as she lay there, sated and drowsy, listening to the beat of his heart slow and his breathing return to normal. And with her lips pressed to his chest, just above the steady beat of his heart, she closed her eyes and drifted back to sleep.

- HEARTBREAK -

Maleficent

I understand you had to leave...
I only wish
you'd left my wings

Stupid Girl

Stupid girl...
Is it any wonder you lay there broken?

You fell
When you said you wouldn't
Loved
When you knew you shouldn't
Hoped
Right or wrong you'd be the one he couldn't
Live without

You weren't...

But let's be honest...
Somewhere
Deep down you knew
You never really stood a chance

Didn't you?
...Stupid girl

Stasis

And so she sat frozen
in her quiet place
the stasis of desolation
and abandoned hope
slowly setting in

as she waited...
for him to return

...waited
for the sun to rise again

...waited
for the whiskey to numb

...waited
for something

...for anything to happen

...anything at all

cathartic enough
to set her free once more

Not Enough Wine

Her heart ached
and overflowed
with too many
painful
nocturnal musings
no amount of wine
could salve

Too many should haves
she could have
let go
but stubbornly refused
she'd take the pain they brought with them
over the emptiness lurking
any day

Oxygen

There was a time
you couldn't breathe
without me near
but then you found
another source of oxygen

Now I'm the one
left gasping
for air

Too Much

Too much for some...

Yet not enough
...never enough

for the one heart
she longed to call home.

Waiting

However long
her heart still waits

Shards

There are times
heartbreak roars
like thunder
across the heavens,
disintegrating on the impact
of angry words and shouts.
Other times
it breaks softly
on the whisper
of the never uttered goodbye
shattering whole
but only splintering off
one tiny shard at a time
as the flame of hope
slowly dies.

Dying Embers

And then came the silence...
and with it
every hope, dream and memory
yet to come,
drifted away
wisps of smoke
floating up
from love's dying embers.

Shifting Sands

The shoreline
to your ocean
ever constant
to your ebb and flow

Don't you realize?
Don't you know?
Each time you pull away
you take a tiny glittery grain of me
when you go

Little by little I'll be less
than before
my shimmery sands
too far out…
too deep to recover

…while you lap and caress
another far off distant shore

Unrequited

And then comes the moment
desolation descends
tears threaten
and your heart bleeds
love unrequited
for no other good reason
than you knew better

...but fell anyway.

Forever Branded

Smoldering
in the ashes
of her undoing
redemption
a distant hope
as yearning
for what was
yet can never be again
slowly burns
a deeper hole
in the space
where his memory lives
forever branded
upon her heart

Numb

Show me what you mean
when you say
"Don't think. Just feel"

I want to...
Need...
to do just that
even if the outcome
is excruciating

Any degree of pain is welcome
to this numb
and frozen wasteland
of my soul.

The Truth

She believed in love
...she always would
she simply
no longer believed
in him

and that
realization
was the dagger
that tore
into her soul

Poison

Memories of him
wound their way
through her bloodstream
consuming her
with deliberate intent
tearing at her soul
until there was nothing left

Quietly killing her
like the slow-acting poison
she'd so willingly devoured

Homeless

You turned my heart
into
blackened
crumbling ash
and left me
broken
in its ruins
Eventually
I'll rebuild
but you...

How does it feel?

Homeless
once again
...as always

Real Man Wanted

Pay no attention
to the mess
you left
behind...

It's nothing
a good hard fuck
from a real man
won't help tidy up

Dismissed

Don't say you love me
then walk away
leaving behind
the consolation prize of friendship
because frankly, you sucked at that

Just go
be gone
get on with whatever needs doing
I might miss you for a time
but not for long

Even with all your edges
and dark shadows
guys like you are all too common
for a girl like me

I'm not like all the others
that was your first mistake

But I guess you were
and that was mine

Vitriolic Fashion Week

In a world
where
vile words
profanely spewed
pass as poetry

where
bloodletting of the innocent
is the accepted past time
of the self-anointed nouveau riche

and where
ugliness and angst
are paraded daily down runways
as the season's most fashionable new black

What hope does a gentle soul have?

Tar

I'm trapped
by your memory
insidious
and sticky
slowly
dragging me down
enveloping me
in a smothering darkness
from which
there is
no escape

The Key

Her heart
once again
locked down
seeking
the safety
and solace
of her quiet space
she retreats
gently
shutting the door behind her
but not before
hanging her dreams
on a latch just outside
in hopes
for another to find
and set free
once more

Acknowledgement

To Lydia Michaels, my friend, mentor and most favorite author of all time. This wasn't necessarily the book I'd planned to release as a fledgling writer, but your nonstop encouragement played a huge part in getting me here. The day you liked one of my poems, I knew I was onto something. Love you!!

To the many friends I've made over the last few years on that wacky social media site Facebook, especially Carla Dragon and Doris Barnes. From the bottom of my heart, I cannot express how much I love and value your friendships. Carla, aka Carlos, I'll road trip with you anytime, as long as you promise to watch for trees better when I'm backing up. And Doris, you are simply a walking, talking blessing in my life. I love you both. I love you all.

To J Blu, your quiet strength, unfailing support and faith in me even when others would have you believe otherwise means more to me than you'll ever know. Thank you for your wisdom and for teaching me to breathe when the world gets sideways. Mwuah!

And finally…

To Alan Walker, my poetry mentor, sounding board, collaborator, second set of eyes and most importantly, my best and dearest friend. Thank you for all the time you've spent, and all the encouragement you've showered upon me. You are the best gentleman friend a gypsy girl could ask for. Oh, and get ready, Poet. You're next! <4

About the Author

Fiona Summerville is a contemporary and romantic suspense writer who also dabbles in poetry.

She is a big city, Southern California girl transplanted to a small town in Texas, the location of which she affectionately refers to as "smackdab in between Podunk and Bumf---," where she lives with her husband and a menagerie of furry, perpetual two year olds.

Before deciding to chase down her dream of being a writer, Fiona made her way through the legal and corporate worlds in stilettos and pencil skirts, as both a Legal and Executive Assistant. Each career was fulfilling in its own unique way, but the call of her muses finally won out, and once she settled in Texas, she began writing in earnest.

As a lover of words, she is a great fan of all forms of writing, but never thought herself concise enough to contemplate writing poetry. It wasn't until she and her family were faced with series of serious medical crises that the Poet Muse emerged.

Her first book, *Only Dark Around the Edges* is the collection of the poetry, prose, quotes and short stories that resulted from letting her Poet Muse run free. She is also working on the first book in a romantic suspense series set in her favorite city of New Orleans, as well as a romantic thriller nestled in the quaint Eastern seaboard town of Mystic.

When she's not writing, she can be found out with her horses or sipping on a glass of wine while getting lost in a spicy novel by one of her favorite authors.

You can find her lurking on the following social media sites:

Facebook: facebook.com/FionaSummerville
Twitter: @Fiona_S_Author
Instagram: @fiosummerville

51528666R00132

Made in the USA
Charleston, SC
24 January 2016